Gymnastics Drills for the Walkover, Limber, and Back Handspring

This book includes drills and strength exercises that have been used with Karen's athletes for many years.

Although the drills, when done correctly have proven challenging to gymnasts of all levels, they are most useful to the developing gymnasts in levels.

As the owner of a gymnastics training facility for nearly ten years and a gymnastics coach for 25, Karen has spent thousands of hours coaching, teaching skills through progressions, drills, strength, and flexibility.

She considers it a privilege to have worked at Karolyi's Gymnastics Camp in Texas for seven summers as well as at US Gymnastics Training Camp held in Massachusetts and International Gymnastics Camp in Pennsylvania for ten years of Holiday Clinics. Working at these camps along with working for Paul Spadaro and attending many USA Gymnastics events such as Regional Congress and the National TOPS Training Camp have all been contributing factors to her vast knowledge of the sport. Karen has great appreciation for all those who were so generous with their knowledge, especially Paul Spadaro, Bela Karolyi, and Martha Karolyi.

Gymnastics Drills and Conditioning
Please spot your gymnast for these drills!

Walkover and Limber

5	Wall Climb
7	Wall Climb to Bridge
9	Bridge
11	Slide Back
13	Shoulder Press
15	Reach Up and Back
17	Reach Up and back From Knees
19	Hip Flexor Exercise
21	Reverse Wall Climb and Kick Over
23	Tic Toc with Block
25	Walkover or Limber from Mat
27	Partner Standing Stretch and Strength
29	Kneeling Split Stretch
31	Hip Flexor Stretch

Back Handspring

35	Fall Back
37	Sit and Fall back
39	Sit, Lean, and Jump
41	Handstand and Fall to Hollow
43	Handstand, Extend Shoulders, Fall to Hollow
45	Snap Down\Chest Up
47	Slide Down and Snap to Hollow
49	Octagon Limber
51	Back Limber to Hollow
53	Trampoline
55	Tumble Trampoline
57	Ball Throw

Gymnastics Drills and Conditioning
Please spot your gymnast for these drills!

Wall Climbs

In order to perform a front or back walkover, first your athletes must first be able to perform a handstand because the walkover passes through the handstand, or vertical.

Have your gymnast stand with their back close to a padded wall.

Instruct them to place their hands on the floor/mat approximately 1-2 feet from wall.

Next, have them place their feet on the wall. (Once feet are on wall, belly faces wall.)

After your gymnast is strong enough in that position...

Instruct them to simultaneously walk their hands in towards wall and their feet up the wall towards the ceiling until their forehead touches wall. Be sure their shoulders touch their ears for a good handstand. (Handstand with belly facing wall)

Keeping their arms straight, have your gymnast either walk back out, remaining very tight.

Or keeping arms straight, have them slide their feet down the wall and simultaneously roll out.

Once this handstand is mastered, have your gymnast perform shoulder shrugs (for strength in the position and awareness of shoulder position during handstand) before rolling or walking back out.

Take precautions...the mat must be secured against wall and the inexperienced gymnast must be spotted and watched closely in order to prevent falling.

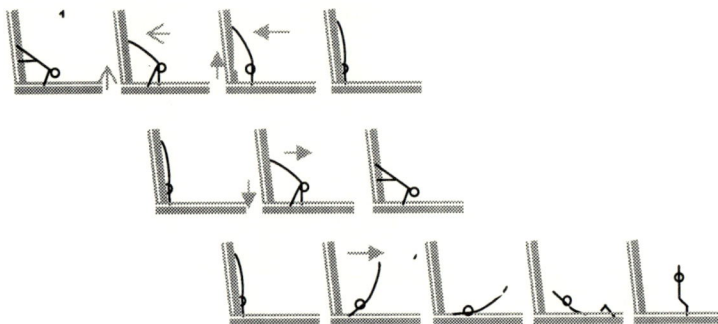

Gymnastics Drills and Conditioning
Please spot your gymnast for these drills!

Wall Climbs to Bridge

After your gymnast has mastered the Wall Climb, allow them to keep their upper body on the wall and drop their feet toward the floor to land in a bridge.

Once they are in the bridge, have your gymnast simultaneously walk their hands up the wall and their feet toward the wall to stand up.

Your gymnast has just performed a Front Limber! This is a basic and very necessary skill for front walkovers and front handsprings!

Take precautions...the mat must be secured against wall and the inexperienced gymnast must be spotted and watched closely in order to prevent falling.

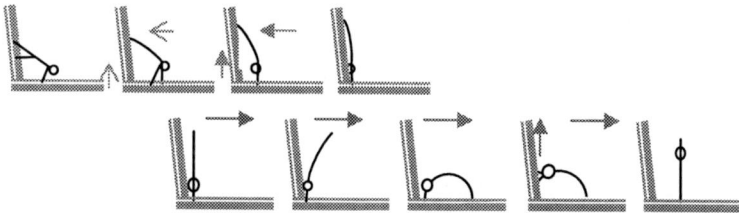

Gymnastics Drills and Conditioning
Please spot your gymnast for these drills!

The Practice Bridges and Stretches

Have your athletes push up to a "bridge" position.

Once their back is off the floor, ask them to press their armpits out to allow their shoulders to be directly above their hands.

A simple way to teach the pressing out position is to have your gymnast perform the bridge facing a wall or mat.

Ask them to attempt to press their armpits toward the wall\mat performing this bridge; concentrating on their shoulders will usually help with the back and front walkovers as well as the back and front limbers.

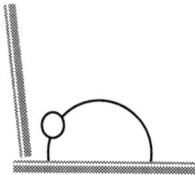

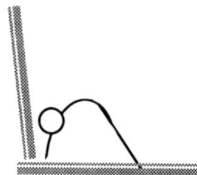

Gymnastics Drills and Conditioning
Please spot your gymnast for these drills!

Slide Back

Once your gymnast is strong enough to hold their self up in an inverted, a handstand, have them lie in a spotting block or mat stack. It should be a block so that it does not move.

Once on your gymnast is on their back, have them put their arms up by their ears. Make sure you inform them to keep their arms straight because they are about to transfer their weight to their hands.

(Take precautions...the mat must be secured against wall and the inexperienced gymnast must be spotted and watched closely in order to prevent falling.)

Instruct your gymnast to slowly slide toward the end of the mat and then toward the floor, reaching with straight arms the entire time. Their arms must be ready to touch the floor then support their body.

Once your gymnast's hands make contact with the floor, they can then transfer their weight to their hands and kick over, step down. They should stand up and finish the skill in a similar manner a back walkover.

Your athlete has just performed the last portion of a back walkover!

It is recommended that your gymnast use a spotting block or trapezoid rather than the octagons or barrels for this exercise in the beginning, when the athlete is new to the sport.

The mat stack will not roll like the octagon; therefore the athlete will have more time and support to transfer their weight to their hands and then feet.

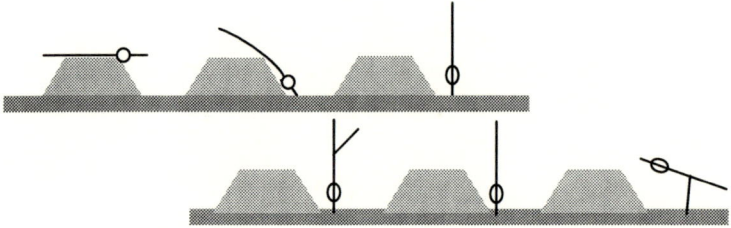

Shoulder Press Stretch

Have your gymnast push up to a bridge with their feet near a stable spotting block.

Once they are in a bride, have them lift their feet to place them on the block.

Once their feet are on the block, instruct your gymnast to press their knees down and armpits out in order to stretch their shoulders. (This is the advanced version of the "Practice Bridge and Stretch.")

Once the Shoulder Press is mastered…
Instruct your gymnast to stand facing the block.

Once they are in position, have them kick to the split handstand and then press their armpits out in order for one of their feet to land on the block as if they are performing a front walkover.

Have them remain in this position long enough to learn where their shoulders are in relation to their hands and the rest of their body.

Make sure you watch your gymnast's shoulders.

The purpose of this drill is for your gymnast to learn how to use their shoulders for a walkover rather than the lower back.

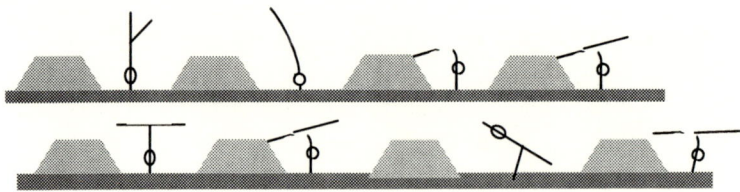

Gymnastics Drills and Conditioning
Please spot your gymnast for these drills!

Reach (Up and) Back

Have your gymnast stand in front of the block or mat stack with their back facing the block\mat stack.

Instruct them to reach\stretch up.

Once they are standing in front of the block, ask your gymnast to reach back and touch the mat with their hands.

Once your gymnast touches the mat, have them return to the standing position.

Once the Reach (Up and) Back is mastered...

Have your gymnast perform the same drill with one leg up in the air as if about to begin a back walkover.

Be sure to instruct your gymnast to lift the front leg up as high as possible without bending their knees.

As their leg reaches the top of the lift, ask them to reach back, keeping the leg up, and touch their hands to the mat.

Once their hands touch the mat your gymnast can return to the standing position keeping their front leg up until instructed to lower it.

This drill will teach your gymnast to reach back with their leg high and reduce any fear of reaching back to the floor for back walkovers.

On the return or standing back up portion of this drill, it should also teach the last portion of a front walkover. Your gymnast learns how to keep their leg up while going from the arched position to the standing position.

It may be easier for your gymnast to return to the standing position if they are reminded to straighten the supporting leg and pull in the abdominal area while attempting to stand back up.

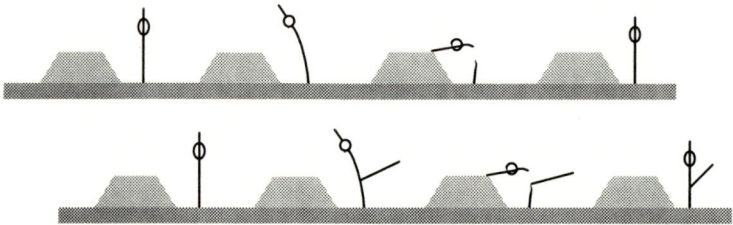

Reach (Up and) Back from Knees

Have your gymnast kneel on the floor with their buttocks off their feet.

Instruct them to reach up. Their arms should be straight and shoulders should be touching their ears.

Next have them press their hips slightly forward and reach back for the floor.

Instruct your gymnast to touch their fingertips to the floor.

Once your gymnast touches the floor, instruct them to press their hips forward, keep their arms on their ears, and return to the starting position.

Their legs can be shoulder width apart or closer together, depending upon their level and their confidence with reaching back. The closer the knees are to each other, the more control necessary.

Once mastered, have your gymnast perform the drill with one leg in front to more closely simulate a walkover rather than a limber.

It is important that your gymnast keeps the top of their thighs together for this drill, even with one leg in front, so that they remain in line.

If your gymnast has a fear of reaching back, even while on their knees, place a small mat or block behind them and progress to lower blocks\mat stacks for them to reach and touch.

Eventually, your gymnast should be able to perform this drill without the block. And one day they should be able to reach back from standing!

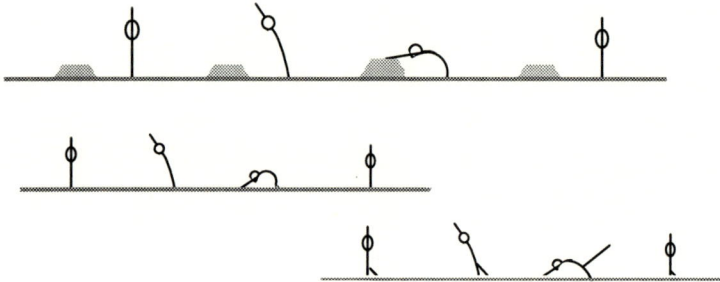

Hip Flexor Drills

These drills should help your gymnast be able to hold their leg up to begin a back walkover or while finishing a front walkover.

Have your gymnast sit on the floor in a pike position.

Instruct them to place their hands on the floor next to their knees.

Keeping their legs straight, feet pointed, and their buttocks on the floor, instruct them to lift both of their legs to shoulder height and then lower back down to the floor.

Have them repeat the leg lift several times quickly.

As your gymnast gains strength in their hip flexor muscles, their hands can be placed further from their body, closer to their ankles.

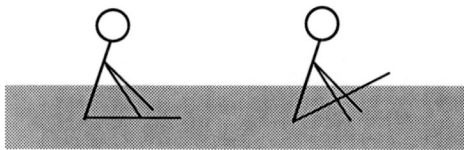

Gymnastics Drills and Conditioning
Please spot your gymnast for these drills!

Reverse Wall Climbs to Kick Over

After your gymnast has mastered the bridge, allow them perform a bridge with their feet close to the wall.

Once they are in the bridge position, instruct your athlete to walk their feet up the wall.

When your athlete's feet are slightly higher than hip height or when they can no longer walk up the wall, instruct them to press their arm pits out and kick over\away from the wall. Your gymnast should finish in the same manner as if they completed a back walkover.

It is important to remind your gymnast to keep their arms straight and their shoulders over\in line with their hands while passing through vertical.

Your gymnast has just performed a Back Walkover, a basic and very important skill!

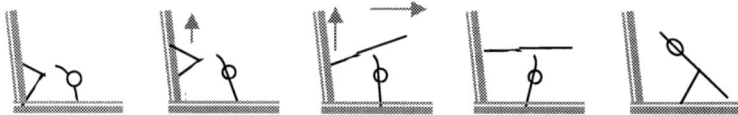

Gymnastics Drills and Conditioning
Please spot your gymnast for these drills!

Tic Toc on Block

Have your gymnast stand in front of a stable spotting block.

Instruct them to kick to the split handstand and press their armpits out, as previously performed in the "Shoulder Press" exercise. Instruct them to attempt to get one of their feet to land on the mat stack or block as if they are performing a front walkover.

Once in the shoulder press position briefly, have them press their armpits back out and slowly bring their front leg back to the starting position to return their front foot to the floor.

Your gymnast has just performed the first half of a front walkover and then the second half of a back walkover.

Instruct your gymnast to move continuously while performing the Tic Toc. They should not hold the shoulder press position. This exercise should help your gymnast learn to pass through vertical in the walkovers.

Be sure to instruct your gymnasts to perform this exercise with their right leg leading once then left leg leading the next time.

Make sure you watch your gymnast's shoulders.
The purpose of this drill is to learn how to use the shoulders for a walkover.

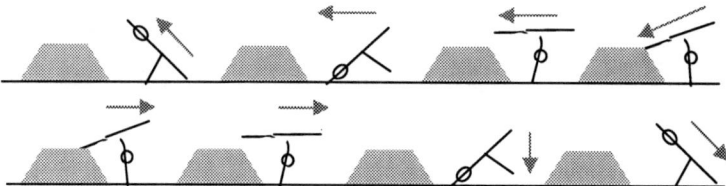

Front Walkover (or Limber) Off Mat

Have your gymnast perform a front walkover by starting out standing on a folded panel mat.

Next instruct your gymnast to kick to a split handstand. If you are working limbers, have them perform the handstand phase with their feet together.

Once in the vertical position, have your gymnast open their shoulders by sticking their armpits out.

Opening their shoulders will help their feet start to drop toward the floor.

Once your gymnast's foot reaches the floor, instruct them to attempt to straighten their knee to stand.

Take precautions...the mat must be stable and the inexperienced gymnast must be spotted.

Due to gravity this will be a very difficult skill for a beginner to control.

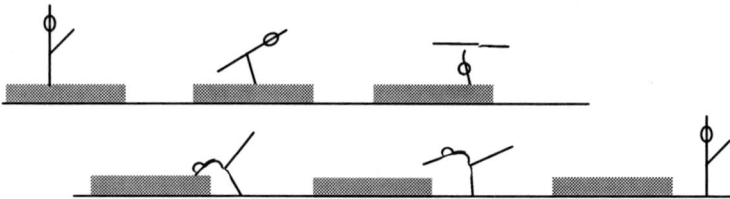

Partner Standing Stretch & Strength

Have your gymnast stand against a wall or in front of the beam. If they are standing in front of the beam, they can reach back, over the beam, and grasp the beam for balance.

Once in position, remind your gymnast that their hips must remain square throughout the stretch.

Allow an experienced partner to stretch your gymnast's leg by lifting one of their legs high enough for your gymnast to feel a stretch in the back of their legs, mostly hamstrings.

Make sure your gymnast keeps their supporting leg straight and hips even. They must keep their supporting foot flat on the floor and both of their legs turned out slightly.

The experienced partner is performing the lifting\stretching for your gymnast for the first 10-15 seconds.

Once your gymnast's partner is done stretching their leg for 10-15 seconds, have your gymnast resist or gently press their leg down during the next stretching phase. This resistance stretching should take place for another 10-15.

After the resistance portion of the exercise, have your gymnast's partner hold your gymnast's heel just lower than the highest stretching point.

Instruct your gymnast to lift their leg up and out of their partner's hand several times quickly. Small leg lifts.

Once your gymnast is able to lift her leg off the partners hand, have her lift and hold for as long as possible. Many gymnasts can only hold their leg at this height for a few seconds.

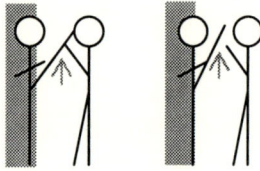

Gymnastics Drills and Conditioning
Please spot your gymnast for these drills!

Kneeling Split Stretch

Have your gymnast kneel on the floor with one leg in front of their body. Once kneeling in front of an experienced partner, instruct your gymnast to reach back and around their partner's legs. Your gymnast will hold their partner's legs for balance.

Once in the starting position, instruct your gymnast to lift one leg in front. Once your gymnast's leg is in front, the partner can grasp the leg and gently and carefully pull your gymnast's leg up toward your gymnast's chest to stretch your gymnast's lower body.

Your gymnast's supporting leg\knee must remain in one position and the hip above their supporting leg must remain straight and open.

Your gymnast's hips must remain square while the partner is stretching your gymnast's legs, they should also be gently pressing their legs forward enough to help your gymnast's hips remain open.

Your gymnast can also perform the same resistance and lifting portions after the initial stretching as was done with the previous exercise.

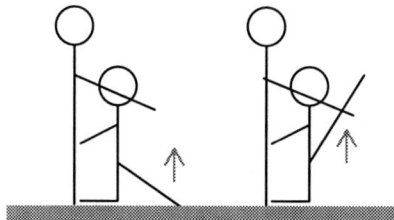

Hip Flexor Stretch

Have your gymnast lie on their back on the vault table, spotting block, or mat stack.

Instruct them to position their buttocks at the edge of the block.

Once in the correct position on the block, have them bring one knee to their chest and hold it close to their chest. That leg should be bent.

Once they have their leg held close to their body, instruct them to lift their other leg above their body with their toes pointed toward the ceiling.

Next, instruct them to slowly lower their relaxed leg so that it is hanging below the level of the horse.

Make sure the leg that is hanging, or being stretched, is lined up with the hip on the same side. Their leg should not be hanging off to the side.

Their hip flexor will be slowly stretched while hanging in this position.

Be sure the object your gymnast is using is high enough off the floor so that her foot cannot reach the floor.

Your gymnast may wear a light ankle weight, depending upon level to get a steady and slightly more intense stretch.

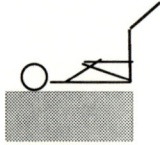

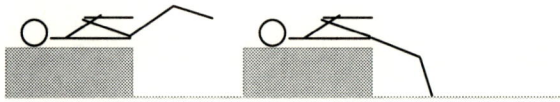

Gymnastics Drills and Conditioning
Please spot your gymnast for these drills!

Many of the previous exercises and drills should be used for limbers as well as walkovers.

The stretching exercises will not only help the walkovers flow more beautifully, they can be used with the more advanced gymnasts for flexibility training.

The next section includes drills and conditioning for the **Back Handspring**.

Fall Back

Have your gymnast stand in front of a very soft wedge mat.

Your gymnast's back should be facing this soft surface.

Once in position, instruct you're your gymnast to remain very tight and raise their arms up next to their ears.

Once tight, instruct your gymnast to fall backwards to land on their back on the soft mat.

Your gymnast must remain tight throughout the falling phase and they should land on their back in a very tight position.

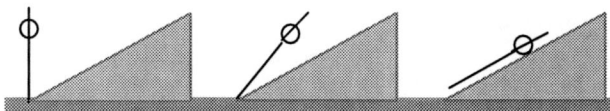

Sit and Fall Back

Have your gymnast stand in front of a very soft wedge mat.

Your gymnast's back should be facing this soft surface.

Once in position, instruct you're your gymnast to remain very tight and raise their arms up next to their ears.

Once ready, have your gymnast bend their knees as if going to sit in a chair, but not quite as low as a chair.

Make sure their buttocks is tucked under and their chest is upright. There should be no arch in the back at this time in the skill.

While in the sitting position, instruct your gymnast to begin to lean back as if performing the fall back drill while in a seated position.

Once your gymnast falls off balance, have them simultaneously straighten their legs and fall the rest of the way to land on the soft mat on their back in a very tight extended position.

Do not allow your gymnast to jump at this point. Have them concentrate on the body positions.

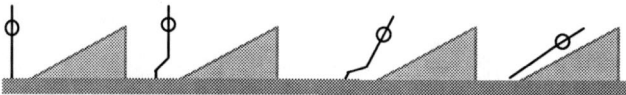

Gymnastics Drills and Conditioning
Please spot your gymnast for these drills!

Sit, Lean, and Jump Back

Have your gymnast stand in front of a very soft wedge mat.

Your gymnast should be facing away from this soft surface.

Once in place, instruct your gymnast to lift their arms up close to their ears.

Once their arms are in place, have your gymnast bend their knees as if going to sit in a chair, but not quite as low as a chair.

Make sure your gymnast's buttocks is tucked under and their chest is upright. There should be no arch in their back at this time in the drill.

While in the sitting position, instruct your gymnast to begin to lean back as if performing the fall back drill while in a seated position.

Once your gymnast falls off balance, have them simultaneously jump and straighten their body to land on the soft mat on their back in a very tight extended position.

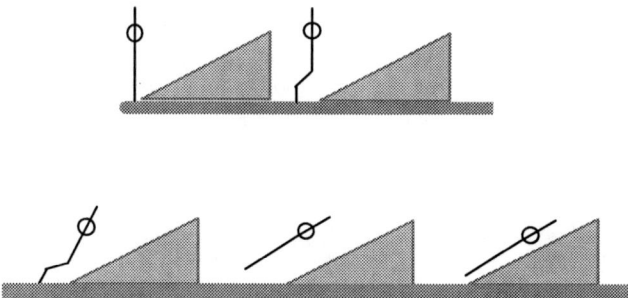

Gymnastics Drills and Conditioning
Please spot your gymnast for these drills!

Handstand and Fall to a Hollow Position

Place a very soft mat on top of the floor exercise area or a matted surface.

Have your gymnast stand on top of the soft surface mat.

Once in the correct place, allow your gymnast kick to a handstand. The handstand must be tight and straight.

From the handstand, instruct your gymnast to simply fall to a long hollow position, not a bridge position. Their belly should be facing the floor, not their back.

If they have fallen into a bridge, they have fallen in the wrong direction.

Once in the hollow position, allow your gymnast to hold the position in order to become accustomed to the position as well as to increase their strength in the long hollow position.

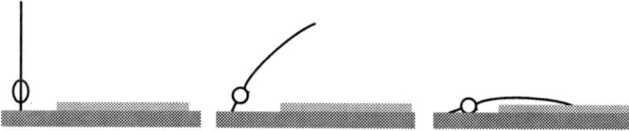

Handstand and Fall from Extended Shoulder Position

Place a very soft mat on top of the floor exercise area or a matted surface.

Have your gymnast stand on top of the soft surface mat.

Once in the correct place, allow your gymnast to kick to a handstand. The handstand must be tight and straight.

From the handstand, have your gymnast extend their shoulders so that their armpits seem to be sticking out. Please spot your gymnast for this drill.

After extending their shoulders, have your gymnast pull their armpits in to initiate a fall to a long hollow position, not a bridge position.

Again, if they your gymnast has fallen into a bridge, they have fallen in the wrong direction.

Once in the hollow position, allow your gymnast to hold the position in order to become accustomed to the position as well as increase their strength in this very important position.

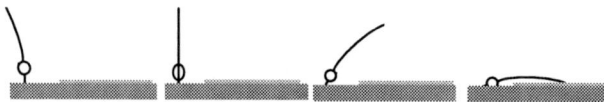

Snap Down\Chest Up

Place a spring board in front of a soft mat with the high end closer to the mat.

Have your gymnast kick to a handstand on the spring board. Their hands must be on the board.

Next have them open their shoulders completely and slightly arch their upper back. Please spot them for this drill.

Next, have them immediately snap\pull their armpits in and then tuck their buttocks under. It will appear as if they are kicking their feet toward the floor if performed correctly.

Remind your gymnast to lift their chest up to a standing position while snapping their legs to the landing position.

Your gymnast should land in a tight standing position with their knees slightly bent, their arms up on their ears, their chest upright, and their buttocks under.

Once your gymnast masters this drill, they can be spotted for a back handspring immediately after the drill to practice connecting the round off or a row of back handsprings.

Keep in mind; it is more of a shoulder movement ending with the chest up rather than a "snap down" drill.

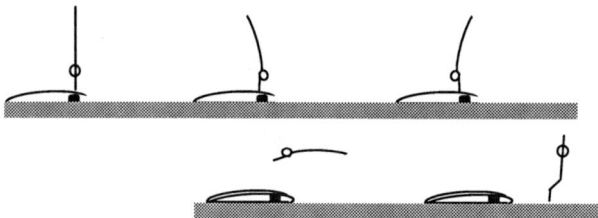

Gymnastics Drills and Conditioning
Please spot your gymnast for these drills!

Slide Down and Snap to Hollow Position

Use a trapezoid, spotting block, or mat stack. Place it on the floor exercise mat or other appropriate tumbling surface.

Next, place a very soft mat 12 – 18 inches from the block.

Have your gymnast lie on their back on the block.

Once in the correct position, have your gymnast slowly slide down reaching for the floor. Be sure to remind them to have their hands ready to contact the floor and then support their weight.

Your gymnast must keep their arms straight in order to prevent landing on their head and for proper technique.

Once your gymnast's hands reach the floor, they will be in an extended handstand position.

Once your gymnast's hands contact the floor, instruct them to shift their weight from the block to their hands.

At this point, your gymnast's shoulders should be completely extended with their armpits opened.

Next, instruct your gymnast to snap their armpits in to land in a long hollow position with their feet on the very soft surface.

Have your gymnast hold the long hollow position for strength and to become accustomed to this position.

This drill specifically trains the shoulder positions throughout the back hand spring.

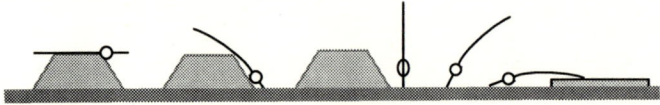

Slow Motion Back Limber over Octagon

Use an octagon or barrel mat. Place it on the floor exercise mat or other appropriate tumbling surface.

Place a very soft mat 12 – 18 inches from the place where your gymnast's hands will contact the floor.

Instruct your gymnast to lie on their back on the octagon or barrel mat.

Once in the correct position, have your gymnast slowly roll the octagon and reach for the floor with their hands.

Be sure to remind your gymnast to have their hands ready to contact the floor and then support their weight.

Your gymnast must keep their arms straight in order to prevent landing on their head and for proper technique.

Once your gymnast's hands reach the floor, they will be in an extended handstand position.

Next, instruct your gymnast to shift their weight to their hands.

Once your athlete's weight shifts completely to their hands, have them snap to a long hollow position with their feet on the very soft surface.

Again, have your athlete hold the long position for strength and to become accustomed to this important position.

This drill also specifically trains the shoulder positions throughout the back hand spring.

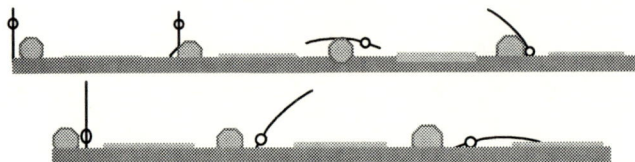

Gymnastics Drills and Conditioning
Please spot your gymnast for these drills!

Back Limber to Hollow Position

Have your gymnast start standing with their arms up by their ears. They must be stretched and tight.

Once standing up tall, straight, and tight have your gymnast reach back toward the floor.

Be sure to remind your gymnast to have their hands ready to contact the floor and then support their weight.

Your gymnast must keep their arms straight in order to prevent landing on their head and for proper technique.

Your gymnast must reach slowly keeping their legs straight and hips open.

Once your gymnast reaches the bridge position, instruct them to shift their weight to their hand and then snap their armpits in.

This motion should bring their legs up toward a handstand.

Once your gymnast reaches the handstand from the bridge, instruct them to snap their armpits in.

This should help them pass through vertical and then to a long hollow position. Bu sure your gymnast's feet land on a very soft surface.

Again, have your gymnast hold the long position for strength and to become accustomed to this important position

This drill specifically trains the shoulder positions throughout the back hand spring. It must be performed slowly.

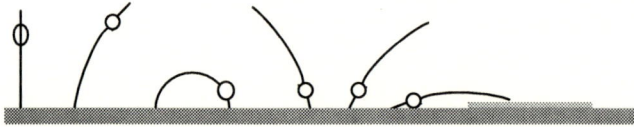

Gymnastics Drills and Conditioning
Please spot your gymnast for these drills!

Take it to the Trampoline

Be sure to spot your gymnast for this drill.

Have your gymnast perform the back limber over the octagon on the trampoline. It should be performed slowly.

Make sure your gymnast lands in the long hollow position and not standing up for safety and technique.

Once the limber is mastered over the octagon, spot your gymnast for a back hand spring to a long hollow position on the trampoline.

You may notice your athlete's hands actually lift off the bed of the trampoline after the shoulder snap is performed correctly and quickly.

Eventually your gymnast will land on their feet without intentionally landing in the upright position just by using the correct shoulder snapping motion!

Make sure there is adequate spotting around the trampoline.

Gymnastics Drills and Conditioning
Please spot your gymnast for these drills!

Take it to the TumbleTrak

Have your gymnast perform back limbers and back handsprings to the long hollow position.

You can have your gymnast perform one back hand spring to their feet and the second to a long hollow position.

Eventually your gymnast will land on their feet without intentionally landing in the standing upright position just by using the correct shoulder snapping motion!

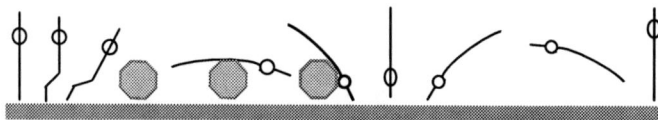

Ball Throw

Have your gymnast start standing in a very tight arch position with a light ball in their hands above their head.

Instruct your gymnast to quickly snap their armpits in simultanrously pull their chest in to a hollow position.

At the end of the snapping action instruct your gymnast to releases the ball.

Your gymnast must finish in a very tight hollow standing position with their arms on their ears . Their hips must remain opened.

Be sure to start your gymnast with a very light ball such as a beach ball and then work up to a medicine ball as their strength increases.

This is another drill for the shoulder snapping action of the back handspring.

The exact opposite body position and throw can be used as a drill for a front hand spring. The athlete must watch the ball leave their hands.

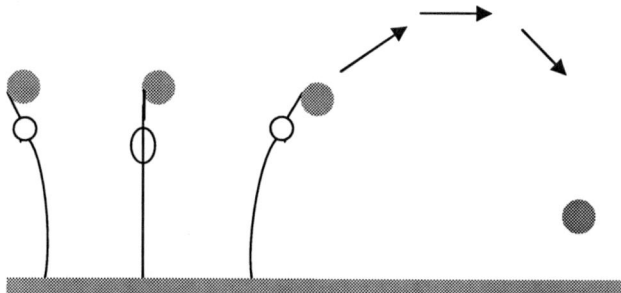

www.GymnasticsDrills.com
Order Form

Item	Price Each	Qty
Over 75 Drills Book	$16.95	
Over 100 Drills Book	$24.95	
Ankle\Foot Exercises	$13.95	
Leg\Landing Pack	$19.95	
Cast HS Drills	$13.95	
Press HS Drills	$12.95	
Running Drills	$13.95	
Dance Drills	$22.95	
Back Handspring Drills	$18.95	
Walkover\Limber Drills	$19.95	
100 Drills & BHS Pack	$43.90	
100 Drills, BHS, WO	$63.85	
100 Drills, BHS, WO, Leg, Ankle	$97.75 (Most Bang for Buck)	
100 Drills, BHS, Leg	$63.85	
All 8 Drills Packs	$122.94 ($136.60 - 10%)	
(Cast, Press, Run, Dance, BHS, WO, Ankle, Leg)		
100 & All 8 Packs	$145.40 ($161.55 - 10%)	
FAQ's Book $14.95		
100 Drills & FAQ's Book $39.90		
100, FAQ, & All 8	$158.85 ($176.50 - 10%)	
Journal	$12.95	

Total

Shipping Calculations for Books, Grips, and Leotards

Cost of items	Inside USA	Outside USA
$0.01 – $24.99	$4.75	$15.00
$25.00 - $39.99	$6.50	$18.00
$40.00 - $64.99	$8.75	$22.00
$65.00 - $134.99	$10.00	$26.00
$135.00 - $159.99	$15.00	$30.00
$160.00 +		Call for shipping quote

Please make check payable to: Advertising Works

Mail to: Advertising Works 32 Algerine Street, Berkley, MA 02779

Name _____ Club Name _____ .
Billing Address _____ .
Shipping Address _____ .
Billing Phone _____ Alt Phone _____ .
Order Total (Amount to be applied to Charge Card or on Enclosed Check) _____
Charge Card Number _____ .
Type of Charge Card _____ Exp Date ____ Security Code (on back) ___ .
Signature _____ .

Printed in the United Kingdom
by Lightning Source UK Ltd.
121193UK00002B/171